# KEITH PIRT COLOUR PORTFOLIO

# GRANTHAM

## Keith R. Pirt

## Compiled by Nick Pigott

*BOOK LAW PUBLICATIONS*

The spark that fired the passion! By a remarkable coincidence, a small meadow at Peascliffe, a couple of miles north of Grantham, was a favourite haunt in the late-1950s and early-1960s of both photographer Keith Pirt and a local lad named Nick Pigott – on whom the trains made such an impression that he went on to become Editor of Britain's top-selling rail journal, *The Railway Magazine* (see Introduction on the facing page). In this idyllic scene, spring flowers are in abundance as A1 Pacific No. 60117 BOIS ROUSSEL passes with the up QUEEN OF SCOTS Pullman on a glorious day in May 1960. *BLP – E1007.*

*Note: In order to provide traction and location variety, the photographs in this book have been placed in approximate chronological order, starting with 1959 and running through to 1962.*

*(Cover Picture)* — see page 33

*First published in the United Kingdom by Book Law Publications 2010*
*382 Carlton Hill, Nottingham, NG4 1JA*
*Printed and bound by The Amadeus Press, Cleckheaton, West Yorkshire*

# INTRODUCTION

Grantham is a medium-sized market town in south Lincolnshire with a long history dating back to Saxon times. Its position on the Great North Road brought trade and wealth for many centuries, but its fortunes really began to soar with the coming of the railways in the mid-19th century.

The first line to enter the town was built by the Ambergate, Nottingham, Boston & Eastern Junction Railway and ran from Nottingham to a station by the old canal wharf, opening in June 1850. That was followed in August 1852 by the opening of the Great Northern Railway's Peterborough to Doncaster main line and, with it, a new station a quarter of a mile south-east of the old one. By the middle of that decade, the GNR had established engine and carriage sheds next to the new station, along with goods yards on both sides of the main line.

The facilities enabled steam locomotives and their crews to be replaced by fresh engines and men for the next leg of their long-distance journeys north or south. The town thus became an important staging point and much infrastructure grew up in the Spitalgate area of the town, including houses for the drivers, firemen, signalmen, shunters, porters and many other staff upon whom the trains depended.

As time went on and locomotives and trains became longer and heavier, Grantham grew in importance and the GNR opened other lines, including ones to Sleaford and Lincoln in 1857 and 1867 respectively and a service to Leicester via Bottesford in the early-1880s (this latter partly in conjunction with the London & North Western Railway). Ultimately, the station was provided with five platforms to accommodate all those services, including two north-facing bays.

The motive power depot expanded too, gaining a second four-road shed to the south of the existing one in 1897.

The discovery of ironstone in the rolling countryside around the town and the growing demand for steel began to generate much extra freight traffic in the area thereafter and even necessitated the opening of several freight-only branches, including one from High Dyke to Colsterworth in 1917/18.

Grantham remained at that level of activity well into the nationalised British Railways era when the Leicester and Lincoln services were withdrawn and modern diesel locomotives rendered the practice of engine-changing unnecessary. The shed duly closed in September 1963 and was demolished the following year, and the goods and ironstone services were gradually run down so that by the 1980s, the passenger station (by then reduced to four platforms) and a couple of old granaries were pretty much the only major railway buildings left in the town centre. Even the original down-side platform buildings disappeared with electrification of the East Coast Main Line in the latter part of that decade.

This book deals with happier times when the engine shed was still open – and I am delighted to have been invited to compile it. For Keith Pirt was one of my editorial contributors and his superb colour photos of the Grantham area date back to 1959 – the very year in which my own lifelong rail passion was sparked by the sighting of A4 No. 60026 MILES BEEVOR on a northbound express in the town.

Although Grantham may no longer be the spotters' mecca I remember so well, it is still an important point on the inter-city map of Britain . . . and long may it remain so!

*Nick Pigott, Editor of The Railway Magazine*

It is perhaps appropriate that we should begin with a locomotive bearing the name of a man whose genius helped to make Grantham such a popular venue for rail enthusiasts. Sir Nigel Gresley was the chief mechanical engineer of the London & North Eastern Railway and his magnificent streamlined A4 Pacifics began to appear from 1935 onwards. Unfortunately, colour photography was in its infancy in those days, so very few decent shots exist of the so-called 'Streaks' in their original silver, garter blue or apple green LNER liveries. By the time Keith Pirt was active with his camera in the late-1950s/early-1960s, the whole class was wearing British Railways' attractive Brunswick green, as illustrated in this marvellous study of King's Cross shed's No.60007 SIR NIGEL GRESLEY basking in the sun on Grantham motive power depot in July 1959. The Pacific will shortly leave the yard to work an express back to London; its tender is full (almost too full, in fact!) and the fireman has the injector on to ensure the boiler is topped up prior to departure. In stark contrast on the right is a grimy local freight engine – O2 class 2-8-0 No.63923. It is sobering to think that the spot on which Keith stood to take this picture now lies in someone's back garden. How are the mighty fallen! *BLP – E40.*

Mention the East Coast Main Line in the steam age and most people immediately conjure up glamorous images of streamliners . . . but besides the passenger and general goods work that characterised most railway towns, Grantham was blessed with a large number of trains conveying a local speciality – ironstone. This mineral, also known as iron ore, was discovered in vast quantities in the hills to the north and south-west of the town and several mining companies began quarrying it and sending it by rail to Scunthorpe and other steelworks in the UK. To access the quarries, branches were laid in several locations along the Grantham-Lincoln line between Honington and Leadenham, from the Grantham-Nottingham line in the Belvoir district and from the ECML at High Dyke, just north of Stoke tunnel. The latter was the largest and best-known of the operations, involving the building by the Great Northern Railway of a single-track line to Colsterworth and beyond, along which main line locos worked from Grantham in order to drop off empty wagons and collect loaded ones from the exchange sidings. In the latter years of BR steam, such trains were primarily worked by ex-GNR O2 class 2-8-0s, but occasionally an O4 of former Great Central Railway pedigree would turn up. Such a veteran – in this case, a member of the O4/8 sub-class – is seen clanking north towards Peascliffe tunnel with a loaded train on a late summer's evening in June 1959. *BLP - E1095.*

The genesis of the famous A4s lay in a design Nigel Gresley had produced for the Great Northern Railway back in 1922 – the A1 Pacifics. Not to be confused with the later Peppercorn A1s illustrated on other pages of this book, the Gresley A1s were later modified to become the superb A3s (epitomised today by the world-famous FLYING SCOTSMAN) and it is one of that celebrity's classmates – No.60112 ST SIMON – that we see in this illustration of an up express at Grantham in May 1959. Although physically constructed by the LNER, ST SIMON was one of a group of twelve engines generally known as 'the GNR batch' and was introduced to traffic as an A1 in September 1923 – just nine months after the formation of the LNER. The tender to which it is attached in this May 1959 photo is a GNR-style version fitted with coal rails. The engine is also sporting a double-chimney; with the exception of HUMORIST, which was so equipped in 1937, such chimneys were fitted to the rest of the A3 fleet in the late-1950s and resulted in improved performance and thereby extended lease of life. No.60112 was, in fact, the second member of the class to be fitted with such an accoutrement by BR, in July 1958. *BLP – E386.*

So skilful was Sir Nigel Gresley as a locomotive designer that he managed to produce a Prairie with almost as much pulling power as some of the Pacifics. The haulage feats and versatility of his V2 class mixed traffic 2-6-2s were so great that during the dark days of 1939-45, they became known by the LNER as "the engines that won the war" – an accolade they shared with the famous Stanier 'Black Five' 4-6-0s of the neighbouring LMS Railway. Although they were often to be seen pounding through Grantham on fast fitted freights, V2s were regular sights on passenger trains in the area too and no shed foreman would hesitate to diagram one to a top link express if no Pacific was available. In this scene in Grantham shed yard in June 1959, the fireman of No.60837 stands atop the tender, wrestling with the water crane before the loco goes off shed for its next turn of duty. Grantham depot was established back in the 1850s and at its peak possessed eight covered roads, a lifting hoist and a mechanical coaling plant. From 1950, it also boasted a turning triangle, installed to replace a turntable that had become defective. Its importance as a major depot and strategic point on the East Coast Main Line was recognised under the BR shed-coding system in the early-1950s when it was given the prestigious code of 35B, but depot reorganisation at the end of that decade saw it demoted to 34F. Even so, it remained far, far busier than the majority of 'F'-rated facilities in the country until its closure in September 1963 and subsequent demolition. *BLP – E1298.*

The town of Grantham lies in a hollow surrounded by limestone hills and escarpments. This caused the Victorian railway builders to construct tunnels in order to get their lines into the town from three sides – north, south and west. Two of the structures – Peascliffe tunnel and Gonerby tunnel – are close together but on different lines: Gonerby on the Nottingham branch and Peascliffe on the East Coast Main Line to Newark. The third tunnel was located near Stoke Rochford, five miles to the south of Grantham. In this photograph, we see the south portal of Peascliffe tunnel, the scorched sides of the cutting telling us that this is midsummer. The tunnel was 967 yards long and lay roughly halfway between Barrowby Road Junction and Barkston Junction. It was a favourite haunt of Keith, who on this glorious July 1959 evening must have been especially excited, for he has captured an A4 he had personally never seen before in this neck of the woods – the North Eastern Region's No.60020 GUILLEMOT, whose shabby external condition is a poor advertisement for its home depot of Gateshead. The reason for this will become apparent later in the book. *BLP – E547.*

From a 21st century viewpoint, it may be difficult to comprehend that the town of Grantham was once a hive of heavy industry. Where today there are retail stores, car parks and housing estates once stood engineering works, foundries, factories, engine sheds and goods yards. With the town also being a major engine-changing point in the steam era, industrial operations went on night and day and the sound of loco exhausts and clanging buffers could be heard all over the town on the still night air. To handle the huge amounts of freight traffic generated by the local goods and parcels depots, Grantham MPD possessed a sizable fleet of shunting engines over the years, including a small number of powerful N2/2 class 0-6-2 tanks, such as No.69560, seen here piloting the down yard in June 1959. No.69560 had become a Grantham loco that month but did not enjoy a long stay and was withdrawn for scrap in October 1960. A classmate, No.69523, was rescued by the Gresley Society in the early-1960s and today survives in working order as apple green-liveried GNR No.1744. *BLP – E407.*

In the locospotting heyday of the 1950s and '60s, Grantham was a magnet for railfans from miles around. Lured by the glamour of the Pacifics, the excitement of non-stop expresses, the fascination of loco-changing and the attraction of named trains, enthusiasts young and old would flock from areas such as Sleaford, Boston, Lincoln and even the large city of Nottingham, whose own enthusiasts were somewhat underprivileged when it came to 4-6-2s and high-speed non-stops. In this May 1959 scene at the north end of the station, 'gricers' of both the adult and short-trousered variety can be spotted as A3 No. 60085 MANNA runs in with a London-bound express. This double-chimneyed Pacific would be a particular attraction for visiting enthusiasts from "the sticks" for its home depot was the north Tyneside shed of Heaton and it was therefore likely to be a 'cop' for many of them. *BLP - E520.*

As steam locomotives go, this one could be described as a bit of a 'brute'! It is an A5 class Pacific Tank and such machines could be seen at Grantham until circa 1960. Weighing more than 85 tons and among the largest and heaviest tank engines to work for British Railways, they had been designed in 1911 by the Great Central Railway's locomotive superintendent, John Robinson, and were inherited by the LNER upon its formation in 1923. No.69814 has worked into Grantham's platform 5 (today's platform 4) chimney-first on a service from Nottingham Victoria and although that wonderfully atmospheric 'cathedral of steam' in the city of Robin Hood had originally been shared by the GNR and GCR, engines of the latter company's pedigree would not normally have worked the Grantham branch in the LNER era. In later years, however, they began to be dispersed beyond the strict confines of the ex-GC routes. No.69814 is waiting to return to Nottinghamshire bunker-first as tank engines working local services were rarely turned. *BLP – E748.*

Back in 1959, nobody had the slightest notion of what Fate held in store for this locomotive. As BR No. 60103, it was just one of 78 A3s on BR's books and the rather workstained condition of FLYING SCOTSMAN at the head of this Leeds-London service at Peascliffe tunnel shows scant regard for the fact that, 25 years earlier, it had been the first steam locomotive in the world to officially break the 100mph barrier. Fortunately, Retford businessman Alan Pegler had a more developed sense of occasion than those entrusted by the State with the selection of locos for the National Collection and, in 1963, bought the icon for the then princely sum of £3,000. In so doing, he not only saved it from the clutches of the scrapman but made the engine even more famous by launching it on a new career as No. 4472 (its former LNER number). Preserved in LNER apple green livery, it has since visited or passed through Grantham numerous times, both in the 1960s before its ill-fated tour of North America, and since its return to the UK in 1973. Twice in the 1950s, Grantham was FLYING SCOTSMAN's home depot and it's not widely known that the world's most famous loco was again based in the area in the mid-1970s. At that time, it was owned by Sir William McAlpine and was housed in a former ironstone locomotive shed at Market Overton, Rutland – access to which could only be obtained off the main line via the High Dyke branch. Also based there at the time was Great Western Railway 4-6-0 No. 4079 PENDENNIS CASTLE, but attempts to turn the venue into a permanent steam heritage centre came to nought and the two icons moved to other locations. *BLP - E923.*

The 'maids of all work' on large parts of the ex-Great Northern system were the J6s. These reliable, uncomplicated 0-6-0 tender engines were the first types to be produced under Gresley's jurisdiction in 1911, although officially their design was credited jointly to him and his predecessor, Henry Ivatt. The J6s shared goods and light passenger duties with the similar-looking J2s and could often be found on Grantham-Boston-Skegness and Grantham-Nottingham services. In this May 1959 scene, Boston shed's No. 64213 gets under way from Grantham with a five-coach train for Nottingham Victoria. Just two years later, the entire fleet of more than 100 J6s would be extinct. Note in the left distance the tower of St John's church – a prominent background feature in numerous railway photographs taken at Grantham over the years. *BLP - E385*.

The south end of Peascliffe tunnel was often bathed in sunlight until late on summer evenings and was a favourite haunt of Keith Pirt (his archive doesn't seem to contain any evidence of him having ventured to the gloomier and less accessible north portal at all). On one such evening in midsummer 1959, he has captured an up express emerging behind V2 No. 60939 as the shadows lengthen after a glorious day. Note that the loco has no outside steam pipes, unlike classmate No. 60837 on page 7. This is because No. 60939, in common with the majority of V2s, retained its original monobloc cylinder casting to the end of its life. *BLP - E1294.*

Car parks now lining the main station approach road have been built where a saw mill and iron works once stood. Against a backdrop of industrial chimneys, A4 No.60003 ANDREW K. McCOSH runs light engine at the north end of the station while performing an engine-changing manoeuvre between there and the depot. Such moves were very frequent at Grantham until the advent of main line diesels in the early-1960s rendered the practice redundant. No. 60003 is one of a number of A4s that were originally named after wild birds but yielded those attractive appelations in favour of rather long and cumbersome names, most of which honoured dignitaries of the LNER. As No.4494, it had been outshopped from Doncaster Works in August 1937 as OSPREY, but lost that title in October 1942. Curiously, the bird name resurfaced half a century later when political sensitivities surrounding the then regime of South Africa caused John Cameron, owner of the preserved No.60009 UNION OF SOUTH AFRICA, to temporarily drop that name. As 'No.9' had never previously carried a 'bird' name of its own, he chose OSPREY. Clearly, Mr Cameron felt, as many thousands of fellow enthusiasts did, that names such as ANDREW K. McCOSH and WALTER K. WHIGHAM were poor substitutes for the likes of OSPREY and SEA EAGLE. *BLP – E549.*

In steam days, the loaded ironstone trains departing the Grantham area for Scunthorpe steelworks usually ran via the Honington-Lincoln line or the East Lincolnshire line. O2 2-8-0 No. 63940 – one of a fleet of rugged and powerful mineral engines designed by Gresley in his GNR days – is seen in this June 1959 scene returning to Grantham with a rake of empty iron ore tipplers. Note that this O2 had retained its spartan GN-style cab to the end, many classmates having been built or rebuilt with side-window versions. *BLP - E1272.*

Grantham's population has roughly doubled since the 1950s and now stands at approximately 40,000 – a demographic boom that has meant that the fields in this photo have been lost and now lie under the sprawling Manthorpe housing estate. The A4 streaking along the straight section of track near the Gonerby Hill Foot district with a London-bound express is No. 60006 SIR RALPH WEDGWOOD, which, like No. 60003 on page 15, had formerly borne an ornithological name, in this case HERRING GULL. Note that in July 1959, the East Coast Main Line in this area was already laid with flat-bottom track, although it was still fishplated. *BLP - E538.*

The late-1950s saw the line's passenger rolling stock in the midst of a transformation from carmine & cream to maroon. Both varieties can be seen in this June 1959 cameo as A3 No. 60066 MERRY HAMPTON brings a London-bound express past the premises of Lee & Grinling's maltsters. Against the odds, one of these buildings still stands in 2010, although not in its original use. (Note the grain wagon just visible behind the loco.) MERRY HAMPTON, which is in unusually grimy condition for a King's Cross-based engine, began its life as a Scottish and Northern-allocated machine and was shedded at Carlisle Canal roundhouse for a while. It became a Grantham resident for the first time in June 1963, only to be withdrawn three months later. *BLP - E1697.*

Even the most glamorous of ladies sometimes have to roll up their sleeves and do the chores – and 100mph "Streaks" were no exception – especially where the northbound leg of the prestigious 'Scotch Goods' was concerned. This was a fast fitted freight that ran between the goods yards of King's Cross and Edinburgh Niddrie. In September 1956, its schedule was accelerated and included a non-stop run to York. For the next few years, it was almost invariably worked as far as Newcastle by a King's Cross A4 (or sometimes an A1), the Pacific returning with a passenger working the next day. Here we see No. 60003 ANDREW K. McCOSH cantering towards Peascliffe tunnel on a warm June evening in 1959 with the vans swaying and rolling behind its tender. *BLP - E1293.*

Sometimes railway photographs can be mightily deceiving. This one appears to depict *THE ELIZABETHAN* but in fact it's the Saturday equivalent, which was never officially a titled train. The headboard should have been reversed for this working, but the crew occasionally forgot! On weekdays, *THE ELIZABETHAN* was a regular sight in Grantham – one of several named expresses on the East Coast route in those classic days of the 1950s when BR possessed a sense of occasion where such matters were concerned. Running between King's Cross and Edinburgh Waverley, it had started life as 'The Capitals Limited' in 1949 but was renamed four years later to mark the coronation of Queen Elizabeth II. MERLIN was one of only four "Streaks" to remain allocated to the Scottish Region for their entire lives (the others being Nos. 60009/12/31) and it will be noted that it carries a plaque on its flank depicting the badge of HMS Merlin, an Admiralty shore establishment in Fife. Those embellishments were fitted to the engine at Haymarket shed in 1946, initially on the cabsides but later in the centre of the casing. No. 60027 was withdrawn in September 1965 . . . six years after its Admiralty namesake was decommissioned. *BLP - E440.*

Grantham shed's own No.60063 ISINGLASS appears to be in the midst of receiving attention from the shed's cleaning staff in this May 1959 scene, for the boiler, smokebox, cab and tender are in highly presentable condition yet the splashers, nameplate, smokebox saddle and everything below the running plate are still covered in a thick layer of grime. As the diesel era loomed and cleaning staff became harder to come by, it was quite normal for the wheels and motion of steam engines to be neglected, but not so common for the splashers to be left, as those too were painted Brunswick green. This, therefore, is a rarely-photographed combination, made all the more noticeable by the fact that the picture is in glorious Kodachrome (most railway photographers in the 1950s were shooting black & white). Behind the Pacific lies a pile of coal that appears to contain more than its fair share of slack! *BLP – E529.*

The large granary building owned by maltsters Lee & Grinling at the south-eastern end of Grantham station has provided the backdrop for many hundreds of classic photos taken over the years, none more so than this wonderful portrait of A4 No. 60021 WILD SWAN in July 1959. As befits a King's Cross 'Top Shed' Pacific, the loco is glistening in the sunshine as it prepares for the climb to Stoke tunnel, followed by a headlong dash down the bank towards Peterborough and the capital city. Although the leading coach may not, to 21st century eyes, look capable of dashing anywhere, vehicles of such vintage were fairly commonplace in express train formations in the 1950s. The same cannot be said for the black-liveried vehicle on the right of the photo, which was in Departmental service and was a fixture at Grantham for some years, providing tooling and messing accommodation. WILD SWAN had been a Grantham-allocated engine twice in its history (from October 1943 to August 1944 and again from March 1948 to June 1950). It was withdrawn from Peterborough's New England shed in October 1963. *BLP - E871.*

A powerful white exhaust lifting just clear of the train, a well-lit and reasonably clean loco and 'cotton wool' clouds in an azure sky: Some of the main ingredients of a successful railway photograph are contained in this lovely study of A3 No. 60064 TAGALIE leaning to the curve north of Grantham station as it sets off with a down express in June 1960. Keith Pirt was justifiably proud of this shot and described it as "a winner". As the owner of a trackside pass and good friend of many signalmen, he was allowed to stand in places that would be strictly off-limits to any other member of the public, in this case close to Harlaxton Road viaduct – scene of a dreadful accident that befell a northbound express in September 1906 with the loss of 14 lives. The precise details of the crash are beyond the remit of this book, suffice to say that its cause remained a riddle for many years until new evidence unearthed by *The Railway Magazine* in 2006 finally resulted in a solution to the mystery. *BLP - E459.*

In this magnificent study of a pristine Pacific being carefully prepared for duty on a sunny day in May 1960, the photographer has captured the very essence of life on a running shed in the steam age. The rather acrid smoke drifting from the chimney of A3 No.60039 SANDWICH tells us that the loco has recently been lit up and the fireman appears to be about to clamber into the cab, probably to check the state of the fire and see how the boiler pressure is 'coming round'. Meanwhile, his driver is oiling the motion – a vital duty before any steam locomotive goes off shed. From today's rather antiseptic perspective, it is hard to believe that such character-filled scenes were once part of everyday life in Grantham. *BLP – E725*.

The familiar wedge-shaped front-end of an A4 was discernible from a long way off and would often lead to cries of "Streak" from young spotters long before the suspect eyesight of more mature observers could make out what was coming! In this classic shot, taken from the 'business side' of the fence at Peascliffe, the graceful lines of No.60017 SILVER FOX are seen to powerful effect as it gets into its stride after calling at Grantham with a late afternoon northbound express in June 1960. Note how the driver, whilst keeping a wary eye on Keith, seems relaxed at the sight of a cameraman standing so close to the ballast (a far cry from the situation in today's health & safety-obsessed society). Like all serious friends of the railway, Keith had enormous respect for the speed and power of trains and knew how to obtain dramatic photographs without ever placing himself in a position that would imperil himself or others. *BLP - E152*

A class of locomotive not so far covered on the pages of this book, apart from on the frontispiece, are the Peppercorn A1 Pacifics. Made famous by the completion of a brand new example – No. 60163 TORNADO – in 2008, the A1s were common sights at Grantham in the 1950s and early-1960s, handling crack expresses turn-and-turnabout with the older Gresley and Thompson 4-6-2s. In fact, between the late-1940s and mid-1950s, no fewer than 18 of the locos (including four brand new ones) were allocated to Grantham MPD – confirmation of the town's importance on the national railway map. One of those 18 was No. 60123 H.A. IVATT, which was shedded at what the local railwaymen called 'the Loco' in 1950. A decade afterwards, by which time it was allocated to Copley Hill in Leeds, it is seen near Belton Lane bridge with the up *QUEEN OF SCOTS* on a warm day in June 1960. The *QUEEN OF SCOTS* was one of the luxury Pullman expresses that once graced the East Coast route and the names of its attractive umber & cream liveried coaches found their way into many spotters' notebooks alongside those of the locos that hauled them. The train was introduced in 1928 and, although being withdrawn during the war, was reintroduced in 1948 and lasted until June 1964. The A1s fell foul of BR's manic modernisation policy, the whole class of excellent and still relatively new engines being condemned between 1962 and 1966 – which was, of course, one of the prime motivations three decades later for launching the construction of a working replica. *BLP - E178.*

We have seen the *QUEEN OF SCOTS* on the facing page. Another Pullman that regularly ran through Grantham in steam days was the *HARROGATE SUNDAY PULLMAN*, which, as its title suggests, served the spa town of that name north of Leeds. This was normally an A1 turn and, on this particular weekend in May 1960, it was being hauled by one of the most common members of the class as far as Grantham train-watchers were concerned – No.60123 H.A.IVATT, named after the fabled Great Northern Railway locomotive engineer who gave the East Coast route its famous 'Atlantic' (4-4-2) locomotives at the turn of the 20th century. It is pictured bursting out of the north portal of Stoke tunnel heading for Yorkshire. The headboard is just discernible in the shadows beneath the smokebox door. *BLP – E1333*.

Besides being a talented action photographer, Keith Pirt specialised in static locomotive portraits and gained a national reputation, not only for producing superbly-illuminated studies but for being one of the first to do so in colour. There were few more natural locations for such imagery than Grantham engine shed yard, the reason being that it was on the west side of the line and was thus bathed in beautiful rich afternoon and evening sunshine. Keith exposed hundreds of Kodachrome frames on this hallowed ground and two of the results are seen on this spread. Both depict A4 No.60029 WOODCOCK in May 1960 – the picture on the facing page being notable in that it shows the rear of the locomotive's corridor tender. *BLP – E1617.*

Corridor tenders were unique to the East Coast Main Line and were a product of Sir Nigel Gresley's fertile mind. (His daughter revealed many years later that she knew he was up to something when she walked into the dining room to find him on his hands and knees trying to squeeze between a gap he'd created between the wall and a row of dining chairs!) The tenders were built with a narrow corridor along the right-hand side to enable footplate crews to be exchanged halfway through long journeys without stopping the train. In that way, the LNER was able to steal a march on its LMS rivals on the West Coast. WOODCOCK, built at Doncaster in July 1937, was one of twenty-one A4s to be paired with a corridor tender from new but one of only nine to be matched with such a vehicle throughout its life. At the time of this May 1960 scene, it was a King's Cross-allocated machine and had been coaled at Grantham ready for its return run to the capital. Note the small 'porthole'-type window to illuminate the corridor. *BLP – E1379*.

Dedicated car carrier services were introduced on the East Coast Main Line in the mid-1950s and initially deployed converted CCTs (covered carriage trucks) or GUVs (general utility vans) to accommodate the motor cars while their owners relaxed 'on the cushions' elsewhere in the train. In 1962, purpose-built double-decker vehicles with a higher capacity were introduced and those can be seen on page 86. In the photo above, the original form of the *ANGLO-SCOTTISH CAR CARRIER* is seen leaving the south portal of Peascliffe tunnel in June 1960 behind the world-famous A4 No. 60022 MALLARD – a loco that had been allocated to Grantham depot between 1943 and 1948. *BLP - E902*.

Although this shot depicting the *ANGLO-SCOTTISH CAR CARRIER* was taken from the same spot in the same month as the photo on the facing page, the fact that the grass is unmown in this picture means we cannot be absolutely certain that he 'spun on a sixpence' and fired the shutter immediately after taking the previous one (Keith unfortunately did not often record exact dates). Travelling in the down direction at Belton Lane is V2 2-6-2 No. 60936, one of those that had been fitted with separate cylinders. It had been transferred that very month from Doncaster depot to New England, but only remained at the Peterborough shed for four months, returning to the Yorkshire town of its birthplace in October. Note how the bright colour of the ASCC shows up the faded paint schemes of the rather motley collection of coaching stock on the passenger train. The field on the east side of the line containing the bales of hay has now been swallowed up by the extensive Belton Woods golf course. *BLP - E1622.*

When, circa 1950, Grantham shed's main turntable finally failed under the weight of the massive locomotives it carried day-in, day-out, British Railways Eastern Region decided not to replace it like-for-like but to take advantage of the fact that the railway owned a large plot of allotments and wasteland adjacent to the engine shed and yard. So it was that the Springfield Road triangle was laid and from then until closure of the depot in 1963, remarkable scenes such as this were enacted – effectively in the middle of a field – every day in full view of residents, shopkeepers, motorists and pedestrians. Because there was insufficient space to lay out a standard three-sided triangle, an unusual 'scissors' layout was adopted, in which the tracks crossed over themselves in the middle of the site. The triangle was a favourite haunt of photographers because, on sunny days, its curved nature enabled illuminated broadside shots to be taken at whichever angle was best for any particular time of day. More often than not, crews well away from the gaze of the foreman on this remoter part of the site were also amenable to pausing their locos momentarily for a posed shot or two, especially if a few 'ciggies' had been slipped into their pockets beforehand! Here A3 No. 60067 LADAS slowly makes its way along the single-track 'angle'. *BLP - 447.*

If there was an award for the best non-action colour photograph of the BR steam era, this would surely be a contender. Not only does it portray an immaculate ex-works locomotive in a complementary setting but it depicts a genuine celebrity insofar as No.60102 SIR FREDERICK BANBURY was one of only two Gresley Pacifics to be constructed by the Great Northern Railway. As GNR No.1471, it emerged from Doncaster Works in July 1922 – seven months before its illustrious sibling FLYING SCOTSMAN, which, of course, was the first Pacific completed by the LNER. After the rebuilding of the pioneer Pacific, GREAT NORTHERN, into a Thompson A1 in 1945, SIR FREDERICK BANBURY became the oldest Gresley 4-6-2, but was withdrawn relatively early – in 1961 – without ever receiving German-style smoke deflectors. Apart from a spell on the ex-Great Central system in early BR days, the doyen of the class remained faithful to the GNR section and at the time of this June 1960 photograph was one of the prides of Grantham depot. The wonderful afternoon light not only emphasises the graceful and perfectly-proportioned lines of Sir Nigel Gresley's celebrated design, but highlights the detail of the coal stage and coaling tower of No.60102's home depot. *BLP – E825.*

A large part of the shed yard lay to the south of the station . . . tantalisingly out of sight from the platforms, bridges and other vantage points. At many MPDs in Britain, the only way for enthusiasts to see what treasures lurked in a locomotive yard, if they were unwilling to risk 'bunking' the shed, was to jump on a train and write as many numbers down as possible as the train passed by. Although such ruses were possible at hundreds of depots around the country, the trouble at Grantham was that the tracks between the main line and the shed yard were often used for stabling carriages and wagons – which meant that the objects of most railfans' attentions were all too frequently obscured! This led to enormous frustrations for enthusiasts, especially for those from other parts of the United Kingdom who were simply 'passing through' and didn't have time to make the long and rather circuitous walk round to the shed. Part of the problem can be appreciated in this photograph – a rake of coaches lining the siding on the west side of the main line as A3 No.60039 SANDWICH gets into its stride with an Up express in June 1960. The locomotive's curious name is taken not from a packed lunch (which would be ludicrously incongruous for such a fine machine), but from a thoroughbred racehorse – the winner of the 1931 St Leger. *BLP – E1630.*

It amazed Keith when he discovered in the 1990s that one of his favourite haunts – a meadow on the west side of the line south of Belton Lane bridge at Peascliffe – had, by an extraordinary coincidence, been the very same field in which a schoolboy named Nick Pigott (later to become editor of Britain's best-selling rail publication, *The Railway Magazine*) had spent many happy locospotting days in the late-1950s and early-'60s. He was amused to think that the two enthusiasts might have bumped into each other while walking through the field, little knowing that they would meet again in a professional capacity 30 years later when Keith supplied Nick with slides for publication in the magazine. Consequently, images such as this take The *RM* editor's mind right back to those warm carefree days when a notebook, a packet of banana sandwiches and a bottle of Tizer were all a British schoolboy needed to be in seventh heaven! In fact, just about the only frustration in those balmy, carefree days was the grimy state of most goods engines, meaning that this O2 2-8-0 plodding north over Peascliffe farm occupation bridge with loaded iron ore tipplers in June 1960 has to remain anonymous. (Today this once attractive meadow is a wilderness awaiting the building of yet another housing estate). *BLP - E441*.

It is almost possible to feel the heat of this lovely June afternoon in 1960 as "Streak" No.60010 DOMINION OF CANADA bursts out of Peascliffe tunnel with an Up express. When first built as No.4489 in 1937, this locomotive bore the name WOODCOCK and although it was renamed just a month later (its former name passing to classmate No.4493), its new identity was later to save its life – for it was the reason why the engine was selected for preservation in 1965. Donated by the UK authorities to the Canadians, it was shipped across the Atlantic Ocean, where it remains to this day as an exhibit in the country's national railway museum in Saint Constant, Quebec. Several attempts have been made by UK enthusiasts to repatriate it, but so far the Canadians have stood firm. *BLP – E504.*

Pacifics of the A4, A3 and A1 varieties handled the bulk of top-link passenger services in the Grantham area during the last few years of BR steam in the district, but there was a fourth type of East Coast Pacific – the A2. This class was unusual among top-link express types on the route in that it contained the products of two separate chief mechanical engineers – Edward Thompson and Arthur Peppercorn. The Thompson A2s were divided into three sub-classes – A2/1, A2/2 and A2/3 – while the Peppercorn design was known simply as A2. The Thompson variety could easily be discerned by the fact that the cylinders were set much further back, leaving all four wheels of the front bogie exposed. The locomotive in this photograph, No.60523 SUN CASTLE, was an A2/3, meaning that it belonged to a batch built new in 1946/47 as developments of the A2/2 (which themselves were rebuilds of Gresley's P2 2-8-2s). It is fair to say that the Thompson Pacifics were not as highly rated by former GN-section enginemen as the Gresley and Peppercorn types and consequently they were more common in Scotland and the North-East, with only three ever being allocated to Grantham. SUN CASTLE was one of that trio, although by the time of this Belton Lane photograph in June 1960, it had been transferred north to Doncaster. *BLP – E1678*.

Storming out of Grantham as thunder clouds gather: This powerful image from May 1961 shows why Sir Nigel Gresley's A4s commanded (and still command!) such awe and respect among admirers. Neither is this just 'any' A4 – for it is the doyen of the class, No.60014 SILVER LINK. In the 1935-37 period, the most famous LNER streamliners were the four silver-liveried members of the class – SILVER LINK, QUICKSILVER, SILVER KING and SILVER FOX. Their fame may have been eclipsed in July 1938 by the achievement of younger sister No.4468 MALLARD in breaking the world steam speed record by tearing down Stoke bank (a few miles south of Grantham) at 126mph, but among LNER aficionados worldwide, the four A4s with 'Silver' in their names continued to be held in the highest esteem even after losing their iconic pre-war livery. Rather regrettably, a renumbering scheme initiated during the tenure of Gresley's successor Thompson in 1946 meant that the four senior members of the class would not receive the logical BR numbers 60001-04; instead they became the rather nondescript 60014-17. But quality cannot be masked and in this portrait, SILVER LINK retains a towering presence as it powers away from the station with steam to spare. It has long been considered a scandal in the world of railways that none of the original quartet of 'Silver Streaks' was preserved – and the scrapping of this particularly historic icon at Doncaster in 1963 is considered by many to be one of the great 'crimes' of railway history. *BLP – E379.*

By and large, railways have been friendly places in which to pursue one's profession or pastime over the years and there haven't been too many instances of ill-feeling, but one of the greatest 'wrongs' was perpetrated in 1945 when LNER chief mechanical engineer Edward Thompson decided to rebuild one of Gresley's non-streamlined Pacifics to his own design. It is well-known that Thompson disliked his former boss and many rail historians suspect that there might have been an element of revenge in his decision . . . for although there were at the time at least fifteen unconverted Gresley A1s he could have chosen from, he picked the pioneer, No.4470 GREAT NORTHERN. This was not only Sir Nigel's first Pacific but the UK's first true 4-6-2 (the earlier Great Western locomotive THE GREAT BEAR having basically been a stretched 4-6-0). As such, No.4470 should have been a national treasure earmarked for preservation when its working life was over. Instead, its graceful lines were butchered in a grisly and ill-fated experiment, which, far from 'improving' the locomotive, rendered it an inferior machine that never again attained the heights of its former classmates. With its cylinders pushed right back towards the driving wheels in the style of Thompson's A2s, its over-sized smoke deflectors and its raised angular running-plate in place of the graceful curved splashers of the original version, GREAT NORTHERN (bearing its BR number 60113) is seen passing a district of Grantham known as 'The Grange' as it heads north in June 1961. *BLP - E631.*

The district of Spitalgate lies at the south end of the town and includes in its vicinity the old Great North Road bridge (just visible in the distance) and a prominent cutting. Double-chimneyed Peppercorn A2 No. 60526 SUGAR PALM, a locomotive that spent almost its entire life allocated to York shed, heads south in this June 1961 cameo. Unusually for the steam era, bushes and saplings have been allowed to proliferate on the sides of the cutting – a sign of things to come! *BLP – E634*.

There are a great many enthusiasts who find beauty among the ash and detritus of depot settings – indeed, an Engine Shed Society has even been formed to bring together such admirers – and in this wonderful portrait, it is possible to understand why. A3 No.60059 TRACERY is basking in evening sunlight during what appears to be a peaceful few moments away from the normal hustle and bustle of a main line running shed. Coaled and watered, it is standing over the pits, surrounded by piles of ash, the odd lump of unburnt coal and carelessly-discarded fire-irons half-buried among the ash. A modern health & safety official would identify 'tripping hazards' everywhere, but men were men in those days and if they fell over, they knew they had only themselves to blame! In early LNER days, TRACERY had been a resident of Grantham but by the time of this June 1961 photograph was a London-based engine. *BLP – E1239.*

The south and mid-Lincolnshire district was one of the first areas in Britain to receive BR diesel multiple units (DMUs). These began working some of the services on the now-closed direct line between Grantham and Lincoln via Leadenham as early as the mid-1950s. While this might have been a blow for local steam fans, the enthusiasts were richly compensated by the fact that some of the Grantham-Nottingham branch services retained steam into the early-1960s; in fact, Grantham depot received an influx of Class L1 2-6-4T locomotives for these duties in the late-1950s/early-60s, some not arriving until as late as November 1961. In June that year, No. 67774, which had been transferred to the town just a month earlier, is seen simmering in the shed yard while awaiting its next turn of duty. Note that the engine is still wearing the older version of the BR emblem, which by then had been superseded on most passenger locos, and also that it is carrying vintage paraffin lamps despite being equipped with electric lighting. *BLP - E729.*

With its Grantham shedcode plate (34F) prominent on the smokebox door, A3 No.60054 PRINCE OF WALES – one of the few in the class not to be named after a racehorse (although it had briefly been named MANNA when new) – gets its heavy train under way after taking over from a 'Top Shed' Pacific at Grantham in June 1961. The fireman has just 'put a round' on to get the train up to speed before the favourable gradient into the Vale of Trent begins to make his job easier and his engine is laying what Keith Pirt described as "lovely up-and-over black exhaust". The issue of 'clag' continues to divide those in the rail world – cameramen love it for making the subject even more photogenic (indeed, some have even been known to slip a fireman a few bob to put up a good show!), but most railwaymen abhor it as bad practice and a waste of coal. Note the fellow photographer sitting on the trackside on the extreme right; imagine him being able to do that on a main line in a town centre today without some busybody reporting him to officialdom! Even if he had formal permission to be there, he would probably have to be in possession of a personal track safety certificate and be kitted out in a bright fluorescent orange jacket and a hard hat! How times have changed. *BLP – E597.*

At first glance, this appears to be a standard shot of an A4-hauled express departing Grantham, but look a little closer and you will see that Keith's camera has captured in the background another Pacific, also facing south despite being on the opposite main line! Such apparent oddities occurred when southbound engines were changed at Grantham as the replaced locomotive would reverse 'light' through the station before running onto the shed from the north end. This was a great source of interest to the assembled throngs of spotters – a crowd of whom can be made out on the platform-end next to the light engine. The Up express on this June 1961 occasion is continuing its journey behind a customarily-polished King's Cross machine, No.60006 SIR RALPH WEDGWOOD. *BLP – E856*.

The notes on page 43 referring to the relatively relaxed attitude taken to lineside access in the old days are even more pertinent here, for Keith has taken this photograph from the steps of Barrowby Road Junction signal box itself. The divergence of the East Coast Main Line to the left and the Nottingham branch to the right can clearly be appreciated in the signalman's view of V2 No.60943 as it heads towards Newark in July 1961. Just visible on the extreme right of the picture is a glimpse of the Ambergate branch. At the time of the photograph, this had been reduced to a freight-only siding serving the industries based around the wharf of the Grantham Canal, but way back in 1850 it had been the only railway line in the town, providing passenger services on the Grantham-Nottingham route. Today, most of its remains have been demolished but bridge abutments and a trace of the earthworks at the northern end can still be made out. *BLP – E1642.*

Only eight of the 184-strong fleet of V2s were honoured with names and (apart from No. 60800 GREEN ARROW, which had smokebox-mounted straight plates) they were identifiable from afar as a result of their curved embellishments sitting rather incongruously on their straight running plates. Among the christened few, the best-known – as a result of its extraordinary name! – was No. 60809 THE SNAPPER, THE EAST YORKSHIRE REGIMENT, THE DUKE OF YORK'S OWN. In the last quarter of the 20th century, commercialism in the railway industry resulted in long and sometimes faintly ridiculous names becoming commonplace on locos and multiple units, but in the 1950s and '60s, such a lengthy appellation was a rarity. The loco is seen in the sidings on the west side of Grantham station while visiting from Darlington depot on a warm August day in 1961. *BLP - E677.*

Grantham motive power depot possessed two distinct shed buildings – a four-road shed alongside the south end of the station and another four-roader a few hundred yards further south, adjacent to Springfield Road. This 'new' structure was built in 1897 and, during the last four years or so of the depot's life, became the only shed on the site following the demolition of its more northerly partner. In the early-1960s, it was unusual to pay a visit to the remaining building without finding at least one O2 2-8-0 in or around the vicinity and in this May 1961 scene, the obliging engine is Retford shed's No.63986, which is beginning to show the signs of hard work despite having had a General overhaul and repaint at Doncaster Works just eight or nine weeks earlier. Note the lamp on the shed's corrugated iron roof blazing away in the middle of the day – clearly the wartime exhortations of just seventeen years earlier to "put that light out!!" had been forgotten. *BLP – E812.*

In 1958, BR began fitting the A3s with Kylchap blastpipes and double chimneys. Although these modifications gave the class even better performance and therefore an extended lease of life, they did create a new problem – drifting smoke caused by the softer blast obscuring drivers' forward vision. Earlier experiments with A1-style full-length smoke deflectors and small 'wing'-style deflectors (see facing page) had not proved entirely satisfactory, but it so happened that the King's Cross shedmaster, Peter Townend, had seen 'trough'-style deflectors in action during a holiday in Germany. He therefore persuaded his Eastern Region bosses to undertake trials. The new embellishments were ready by October 1960 and, by happy chance, the first A3 to be fitted with them was a Grantham engine – No.60049 GALTEE MORE, which King's Cross promptly borrowed for a week in order for Peter to monitor the results for himself. So successful were the 'German-style' deflectors in lifting the smoke clear that 55 of the 78-strong class (including all those allocated to Grantham) were equipped over the next two years. In this July 1961 scene south of the station, Grantham's No.60105 VICTOR WILD is sporting its 'blinkers' as it brings an Up express under the Great North Road bridge and past the water tank at Spitalgate. Opinion among enthusiasts as to the aesthetic value of the deflectors was divided: older men who had grown up with the locomotives in LNER days said they marred Gresley's fine lines but other admirers felt they enhanced and accentuated the long, graceful looks of the design. *BLP – E1375.*

If a photographer spends long enough by the lineside, the 'Law of Averages' states that he'll eventually witness two trains meeting right in front of him, but even so, it was still extraordinarily lucky to get two engines of the same class virtually 'kissing smokeboxes' at speed. The coincidence took place in July 1961 when A3s Nos.60067 LADAS and 60048 DONCASTER passed south of Barrowby Road junction. The latter locomotive was one of only four A3s fitted with small wing-style smoke deflectors in BR days (see caption on facing page). Those modifications were not considered a success and, in the cases of Nos.60048, 60061 and 60112, were replaced in 1961/62 with the larger German-style variety. DONCASTER is heading north on the main line; the two tracks on the right of the photograph being those for the Nottingham branch. *BLP – E1641*.

The electrification of the East Coast Main Line through the Grantham area in the late-1980s, allied with changes in local agricultural practices, including a gradual shift from dairy to arable, resulted in the removal of a number of farmers' occupation bridges. One of the most regrettable losses was this handsome and lofty three-arch structure over the three-track section in Saltersford cutting, which in this July 1961 scene is standing sentinel to the passage of an Up express hauled by A1 No. 60115 MEG MERRILIES. Although several A1s were, in East Coast tradition, adorned with the names of racehorses, No. 60115 was not among them, being one of a batch named after characters of the novelist Sir Walter Scott. *BLP - E74.*

Although the future *Railway Magazine* editor Nick Pigott was able to 'cop' many A3s in his youth, he was only lucky enough to 'cab' one of them – No. 60062 MINORU. Here the object of his attentions rests on Grantham shed in May 1961, next to a fellow GN-tendered classmate. Built at Doncaster in 1925, MINORU was a fine thoroughbred in both senses of the word, being named after the winner of the 'Derby' and '2000 Guineas' of 1909, a steed owned by the reigning monarch, King Edward VII. This photo was taken just a few weeks before No. 60062 gained German smoke deflectors. *BLP – E756.*

So far in this volume, we have seen mainly passenger and freight locomotives, due largely to the fact that, in 1959 and 1960, Keith appears to have been selective in how he used the relatively scarce and expensive colour transparency film available at the time. But as anyone lucky enough to have visited Grantham in the steam era will know, there were also a good number of 4-6-0 mixed traffic engines to be seen. In the earlier BR period of the 1950s, B1s, B12s and B16s would have been on the agenda, but by 1961 the older locomotives had largely been withdrawn or transferred away, leaving the Thompson B1s as the staple diet. Built between 1942 and 1952, these were, by general consensus, the most useful of Thompson's designs and they were common in Lincolnshire and neighbouring counties, Grantham shed itself having a number on its books at one time or other. In this July 1961 scene near Barrowby Road Junction, No.61393 is hurrying south with something not seen on the modern railway for many years – a fish train. This one used to run from Hull docks to a goods yard just south of Finsbury Park and was a lodging turn, the engine and crew working to Hull with an ordinary freight the previous evening. It was almost always diagrammed for a King's Cross B1 and was reckoned to be the longest booked duty for the class. *BLP – E1643.*

The majority of East Coast Pacifics were overhauled at Doncaster Works – a vast complex known to railwaymen as 'the Plant' – and an added bonus for local enthusiasts at Grantham would be the occasional appearance of extremely rare locomotives from other parts of the BR system on test runs before being dispatched back to their home sheds on the Scottish or North Eastern Regions. Some of those gleaming 'ex-works' locos would run only as far as Barkston Junction, being turned on the triangle there in order to return north, but others would be diagrammed onto service trains and would thus turn up in the station. One such guest appearance, in May 1961, has brought a Scottish Region Peppercorn A2 to town. Edinburgh Haymarket shed's No.60536 TRIMBUSH (named after the winner of the 1947 Doncaster Cup horse race) is waiting to return to the north on a running-in turn, having left Doncaster paintshop just a day or two earlier. *BLP – E363.*

Using his lineside pass and his friendship with local railwaymen to the full, Keith spent a fair amount of time on the side of the main line near the down yard (how he must have been envied by those confined to the platform!). On this occasion, his privileged vantage point has resulted in a classic image of A4 No. 60029 WOODCOCK on a semi-fast 'stopper' as it gets away from the station and buckles down to the climb to Stoke tunnel in May 1961. A burst of wind has caught the white exhaust, whipping it up ahead of the loco to form almost a natural frame as the train passes some of the many cattle wagons that could usually be seen lined up in the up goods yard in those heady days of the early-1960s. *BLP - E502.*

Moody and magnificent . . . the doyen of the Gresley non-streamlined Pacifics, No.60102 SIR FREDERICK BANBURY, at rest on Grantham MPD in May 1961 – just six months before it was withdrawn and condemned for scrap. Its demise represented a sad and undeserved fate for such an historic icon, for, as the oldest of the A3s and the only one built by the Great Northern Railway to survive in original condition, it is astonishing that British Railways or the State-run national museum services didn't see fit to save it, even if only to retro-convert it back to original 1922 condition. Peeping out from behind it in this picture is a WD 2-8-0, none of which seem to have tempted Keith to devote a separate photograph to during his visits to Grantham. Perhaps compared with some of the heavily industrialised locations he visited in his native North Midlands, there were too many glamorous competing attractions on the main line! *BLP – E358.*

It's perhaps not immediately apparent to the untrained eye, but this is a Scottish locomotive. The giveaway is the light blue background to the nameplate of A4 No. 60031 GOLDEN PLOVER (pale blue being the colour of BR's Scottish Region, just as dark blue was associated with the Eastern Region – although in the latter it was restricted to station and lineside furniture and not extended to locos). Most A4s seen at Grantham had black or red-backed nameplates. GOLDEN PLOVER was one of Edinburgh's finest, being allocated brand new to the city's Haymarket depot in 1937 and staying there for a quarter of a century until being transferred to Glasgow St Rollox for the last three years of its life. It was attached to corridor tenders for its entire career, which made it suitable traction for *THE ELIZABETHAN*, the non-stop East Coast express that ran between Edinburgh and London. According to Keith's notes, this shot south of Barrowby Road in summer 1961 depicts *THE ELIZABETHAN*, but the composition of the rolling stock and the fact that the headboard has been reversed tells us that this is in fact one of the regular Sunday workings for which the 'Lizzie' batch of A4s were diagrammed. *BLP - E931.*

When photographing Down trains restarting from the station, a vantage point favoured by Keith was Harlaxton Road bridge, just to the north of the station. Here he has captured 'supershine' King's Cross A3 No.60061 PRETTY POLLY passing Grantham North signal box in May 1961. As explained on pages 48/49, No.60061 was one of four A3s fitted for a while with 'wing'-style smoke deflectors in an unsuccessful attempt to cure the problem of drifting exhaust following the fitting of double chimneys in the late-1950s. It also bore one of the less fortunate racehorse names and it's a source of regret among many A3 admirers that a member of such a powerful and respected class should be saddled with such a flippant and undignified name . . . made even harder to understand by the fact that this mount didn't even win a Derby. (It has been suggested by at least one irreverent commentator that Gresley as a young man must have once won a bet on it!) *BLP – E589.*

A3 No. 60063 ISINGLASS runs through the station to get from the depot to the Up side engine sidings, where stand-by locos used to wait in readiness for southbound engine changes. At first glance, it seems as though the Pacific is running without lamps, which would have been technically against regulations, but closer inspection reveals a single lamp in the lower central position, indicating a light engine. On the platform in this June 1961 picture can be seen one of the large frames installed at both ends of the station to hold the panels used for sealing off carriage gangway-ends whenever necessary. *BLP - E927*.

This was a rare sight at Grantham in BR days – a reasonably(!) clean goods engine. It's almost possible to feel the radiated glow from the newly-deposited ash on the ground as O2 class 2-8-0 No.63940 simmers quietly at the end of a summer's day. A member of the town's home fleet, it is proudly bearing one of the 34F shedplates that replaced 35B in the national depot code upheaval of 1957/58. Visible beyond the tender of the O2 is the depot's 'shearlegs' hoist. *BLP - E523.*

We now enter the year 1962, one in which Keith Pirt appears to have made at least five visits to the town, compared with just two in each of the previous three years. Clearly, he was conscious that the diesel invasion, although still in its early stages, was starting to proceed at a more rapid pace than previously envisaged. On this occasion, he has eschewed his traditional front three-quarters format and gone for a bold rear three-quarters shot depicting North Eastern Region A3 No.60083 SIR HUGO waiting to leave for London. What immense pent-up power and mechanical magnificence this portrait conveys! Just look at the open firebox, so thoughtfully framed by Keith between the cab and tender sides, and the signalbox nameboard conveniently locating the photograph for anyone finding it years later should his notes ever have been mislaid. Look also at the wealth of detail captured by the high-quality lens . . . the oval brass worksplate, the route availability code on the cabside, the slight limescale staining from the mudhole door, the hint of a steam leak around the 'banjo' dome, and the lubricant around the wheels glistening in the April sunshine. It is said that a picture is worth a thousand words; well, this one says it all about the power and the glory of the everyday steam scene at Grantham in those halcyon days. *BLP – E741*.

With barely a trace of exhaust in the hot August air near Little Ponton, A1 No.60146 PEREGRINE makes light work of the southbound climb from Grantham to Stoke summit. The East Coast Main Line at this point is a three-track railway, the metals on the right belonging to the Up slow, which was useful in keeping ponderous ironstone, coal and other goods trains off the fast lines as they slogged up the gradient (it is still in use today for freights and regional passenger trains). Note the grimy state of this top link Pacific; by 1962, engine cleaners were in such short supply at steam sheds (with the exception of King's Cross – see page 63) that it was often difficult for passengers to tell whether they were being hauled by a Brunswick green locomotive . . . or a black one! The locomotive is also showing a hint of smokebox scorch – see next caption. *BLP – E879.*

We now move to a new location for this book – the south portal of Stoke tunnel. This was just a few hundred yards from the famous Stoke summit, from which expresses were customarily 'launched' down the incline towards Peterborough in the hope of a scintillating run or perhaps to make up time lost on earlier stages of a journey. In this August 1962 scene, Heaton-allocated A3 No.60088 BOOK LAW doesn't look well-equipped for racing, for an ill-fitting smokebox door seal coupled with hard work by the engine has caused the build-up of char behind the door to scorch the metal and produce this unsightly rust colour – a sign of poor maintenance in the dying days of steam. Despite its run-down appearance, the engine soldiered on for another fourteen months, not being withdrawn until October 1963. Some years later, of course, it lent its name to the publishers of this book! *BLP- E709.*

This illustration has deliberately been placed on the same spread as the one on the left to demonstrate an extraordinary contrast in attitudes among shed foremen. It has already been stated (page 48) that King's Cross 'Top Shed' supremo Peter Townend initiated the fitting of German smoke deflectors to the A3s, but not so widely known is the fact that he was also a strong believer in the smart presentation of express passenger locomotives as he felt that gave a good impression to the travelling public. So it was that when other depot foremen were asked to make financial savings and dispensed with their cleaning staff, Peter chose to find savings elsewhere and kept not only his cleaners, but his cleaner-foremen, who were sticklers for discipline. The results could be seen on almost any Pacific bearing a 34A shedplate during the years of Peter's tenure (1957-1961) and his legacy continued for at least another year, as this shot of A3 No.60059 TRACERY in August 1962 (almost a year after its last works visit) proves. Sadly, it was to be withdrawn just four months after this photograph was taken. The gleaming Pacific is rather incongruously coupled to a freight whose first three wagons are humble cattle wagons and, whether it is a trick of the light or not, it appears to have darker boiler cladding at the front. *BLP – E797.*

The British Railways mixed traffic livery of black lined out with straw and vermillion could look most attractive when reasonably clean, as evidenced by this pleasing study of B1 class 4-6-0 No. 61389 at rest in Grantham yard in August 1962. Being built later than the Gresley Pacifics, many of the Thompson B1s were fitted with electric lighting and the steam-powered generator and wiring for this can be noted on the running plate adjacent to the steam pipe with one rather straggly wire leading along the boiler cladding to the footplate. It is interesting also to contrast the functional flat-sided B1 tender with the coal rails and rounded corners of the more graceful Great Northern style. *BLP - E413.*

Anyone who has ever 'bunked' a steam shed knows that you don't leave without checking behind walls too, just to be sure! In Grantham's case, a line-up of interesting motive power was often to be found lurking behind the western wall of the shed, including, on this August day in 1962, New England depot's N2 0-6-2T No. 69568, which (according to the photographer's notes) was in light steam. There is some uncertainty among railway historians as to whether this loco and fellow N2 No. 69529 ever undertook stationary boiler duties at Grantham and the author would be grateful for confirmation. No. 69568 had spent much of its life working the sub-surface Metropolitan lines in the King's Cross area and had thus been fitted with condensing apparatus (one of the large pipes for transferring steam back to the water tanks being visible). Note also another throwback to that earlier role: the two brackets protruding from the smokebox door, which once would have held a destination board stating King's +, Gordon Hill, New Barnet or similar. Incidentally, the old GNR tender on which the N2 is leaning is an internal-user Departmental vehicle, probably a sludge carrier. *BLP - E594.*

The two photographs on this spread make a 'matching pair', for they show the celebrated mileage boards erected just south of Stoke tunnel – one to let passengers know that they were exactly 100 miles from London and the other informing them that they had better start getting their luggage together if they were due to alight at Grantham, as it was a mere five miles away. Passing the latter sign on the two-track section immediately south of the tunnel in August 1962 is V2 2-6-2 No.60966, which is in original condition without outside steam pipes. *BLP – E739.*

The two '100 mile' boards – one on each side of the line – were positioned a little further south of the Grantham ones (see previous caption) and were located after the twin turn-outs that converted the route into a quadruple-track railway at this juncture. The signs make attractive 'props' for the photographer's artistic eye as German smoke-deflectored A3 No.60039 SANDWICH brings its long uniform rake of maroon coaches past Stoke 'box with a London-bound service in August 1962. Note from these two pictures how the signalling of the ECML at that stage was in transition between colour lights and semaphores. Sadly, the mileage signs no longer stand, although a similar metal artefact – marking the point at which MALLARD broke the world record in 1938 – was erected in more modern times a few miles further down Stoke bank. *BLP – E998.*

A classic portrait of A3 No. 60047 DONOVAN at rest in September 1962. That was the month in which the loco was transferred from Grantham to New England (Peterborough), but as the shed codes of the two depots were 34F and 34E respectively, it is not possible with any certainty to tell if this picture was taken before or after the switch. Even more intriguingly, the tender appears to have been exchanged recently, for it is sporting a much fresher coat of Brunswick green with full orange and black lining-out, whereas the engine's green paint has darkened with use and the lining-out is virtually undiscernible. The comparison is especially noticeable on the cabside, yet there is no official record of the tender having been changed that year. On the contrary, the 'bible' of the subject, Yeadon's Register, states that the engine kept the same one from May 1948 until its demise – so was this a local depot initiative using a tender from a recently-withdrawn classmate to replace a faulty one (or was it simply the case that the tender had been cleaned but not the engine?) It would be interesting to hear from any readers who know the answer. *BLP - E683*.

One of the best-known railway locations in the countryside around Grantham was High Dyke. Based immediately north of Stoke tunnel and taking its name from the local term for a nearby Roman road, it was a single-track freight-only branch running parallel to the road for four miles to Colsterworth, beyond which it split to serve the parishes of Stainby and Sproxton. Those villages never had a passenger service, the sole reason for the line's existence being ironstone, which was quarried in vast tonnages in the area and moved to High Dyke sidings (visible in the distance). From there, the loaded tippler wagons were hauled to steelworks in the North and Midlands. The branch survived long enough to be diesel worked (mainly by Brush Type 4s and 2s), but closed in the 1970s. In this shot of A1 No.60119 PATRICK STIRLING speeding past the site with a Down express in August 1962, note the impressive signal gantry that spanned the main line – a feature that has since disappeared but is remembered in countless photos taken by various enthusiasts over the years. *BLP - E318.*

One of the great things about Grantham from the local schoolboys' point of view in steam days was that one of the official entrances to the shed was off a public pedestrian subway under the line – and it was therefore possible for bolder lads to venture up it for a short distance when no footplatemen were coming or going and find themselves standing just inches from the shed access tracks! This August 1962 photograph shows how close some of the boys used to get as V2 No.60862 comes on shed with the driver keeping a wary eye on him. Double-chimneyed V2s were rare beasts – only eight of the 184-strong class were so modified, as late in their careers as 1960/61. In the right distance can be seen Grantham's parish church, St Wulfram's, which at 282ft has the third-highest parish church spire in England. *BLP – E569.*

Keith has clambered above the south portal of Stoke tunnel for this rather dramatic shot of a northbound express about to plunge into the depths of this 880yd long structure in August 1962. Stoke signal box can just be made out on the curve in the distance, as can the 'Grantham 5 miles' signs a little closer as a clean A3 – No.60071 TRANQUIL – hurtles into the subterranean depths with a 12-coach express bound for Newcastle. *BLP – E1371.*

Lying between Saltersford and Great Ponton is a large outcrop of limestone rock, through which the Victorian navvies had to break their way in order to construct the Great Northern's route south of Grantham circa 1850. More than a century later, the sheer rock face retains a dramatic and craggy look as A3 No.60039 SANDWICH puts up a fine white exhaust while charging upgrade with a short southbound service comprising just seven coaches and a van. Unfortunately for King's Cross shed's cleaners, water scale on the firebox sides seems to have undone much of their hard work by trying to match the surrounding geology! *BLP – E453*.

Grantham MPD's 'namers' in the years of BR steam were mostly Pacifics, but between June 1959 and September 1963 there was a notable exception – B1 4-6-0 No.61251 OLIVER BURY – which was a regular in the area during that time and worked all manner of duties. Sporting an SC (self-cleaning smokebox) plate under its 34F shedcode, it is impatiently awaiting the road in Grantham's platform 5 with a Down train on a fine day in August 1962. In June 1963, it was joined at Grantham by sibling loco No.61250 A.HAROLD BIBBY, but both were transferred to Doncaster when the Lincolnshire town's depot was shut down three months later. *BLP – E721*.

The single-storey office building at the south end of platform 2 (now platform 1) has to be one of the most photographed structures of its type in the country, having appeared as the background of countless thousands of photos. Not too many of those pictures depict Thompson Pacifics, however – partly because they were scarcer and partly because not all enthusiasts found them sufficiently attractive. Fortunately for posterity, Keith was not averse to the occasional exposing of one of his precious colour slides on them, especially by mid-1962 when it had become clear that such opportunities wouldn't be presenting themselves for much longer anyway. The result is this illustration of Doncaster depot's A2/3 No.60523 SUN CASTLE calling at the station with a train for the capital in May of that year. *BLP – E982*.

A cracking shot of one of Mr Peter Townend's 'supershine' King's Cross Pacifics as it runs towards Grantham with a train from the capital in August 1962. This pin-sharp scene has been perfectly frozen in time for us, depicting not only immaculate A3 No.60066 MERRY HAMPTON and its long rake of matching maroon coaches, but the rarely-photographed Grantham South signal box and part of the large heavy engineering complex that formerly lay to the south and east of the station, operated by the likes of major employers such as Ruston & Hornsby and Aveling-Barford. *BLP – E567.*

Granthamians were fortunate in that the most famous locomotive in the world was a regular sight in the town. This was, of course, the A4 MALLARD, which, as LNER No. 4468, had smashed the world speed record for steam traction by hurtling down Stoke bank at 126mph on July 3, 1938. The special test train on that historic day had started its epic journey from Barkston Junction, four miles north of the town, and had accelerated through the station towards Stoke summit before beginning its headlong downhill descent through Corby Glen, Little Bytham and Essendine. Twenty two years after that momentous occasion, MALLARD, now renumbered 60022, is pictured retracing its steps through the station as it heads towards the scene of steam traction's greatest achievement. On this occasion, of course, its speed would have been far more modest, although A4s did often touch the 'ton' in BR days; indeed, one, No. 60007 SIR NIGEL GRESLEY, set a British post-war steam record of 112mph on the same stretch of line in May 1959. *BLP - E1612.*

The curved main line between Grantham station and Barrowby Road Junction was heavily cambered, even in steam days, and this shot of A1 No.60153 FLAMBOYANT on a Down working illustrates the way trains used to lean into the curve. Keith rarely 'wasted' precious film on the "infernal combustion" machines that were eliminating his beloved steam traction, but occasionally he had no choice. Such a situation occurred in this August 1962 scenario when a Lincoln-based 'Derby Heavyweight' DMU failed to keep sufficiently out of the way as the A1 bore down on the scene. Mind you, it would have been much worse for Keith if the 'bog-cart' had eclipsed the Pacific! *BLP – E689.*

Imagine driving along the road and seeing this in a 'field' alongside you! That was the experience motorists in Springfield Road, Grantham, used to have on a regular basis as main line locomotives were turned on the depot's triangle (see caption on p32). In this 1962 scene, the world's fastest steam locomotive, A4 No. 60022 MALLARD, is crawling along in reverse as it negotiates its way back to the shed yard via the far end of this unusual scissors crossing. The plaque on the side of the locomotive commemorates the record-breaking 126mph it had achieved a few miles further south of here in 1938. *BLP - E56*.

Keith and other photographers loved Grantham's triangle, because they could get full-bore sun shining onto the side of any locomotive at almost any time of day simply by shifting their position relative to the position of the sun in the sky (assuming it wasn't overcast, of course!). This time the object of their attentions is a machine far less glamorous, yet just as important in its own right – O2 2-8-0 No.63943. It is August 1962 and it has not long been out of works, so not had time to accrue the almost obligatory layers of grime so often associated with these workhorses. The full tender shows that it has been serviced on the depot and is being manoeuvred ready for its next turn of duty. What a great shame none of these robust and ruggedly handsome Gresley locomotives was saved for preservation. *BLP – E544.*

This locomotive is so dirty that most passengers would assume its original paint scheme was black rather than green! In the early 21st century, former King's Cross supremo Peter Townend revealed that he and his opposite number at Gateshead shed used to engage in friendly banter and pull each other's legs about whether it was better to smarten engines up or save money on cleaning costs! Gateshead and most of the other depots in the North-East were by then habitually turning out engines in unkempt condition . . . and readers will doubtless make up their own minds about the merits and demerits of those policies after seeing the photographs on this spread. On this page is A1 No.60142 EDWARD FLETCHER making an appearance in the Grantham area with an Up express bursting out of Stoke tunnel in August 1962. This A1 was at the time allocated to Gateshead's neighbour, Heaton shed, and any Lincolnshire spotter who didn't see it on this day would be kicking himself as the very next month it was transferred even further north – to Tweedmouth! *BLP – E870.*

And this is the alternative to the image on the left! King's Cross A3 No.60110 ROBERT THE DEVIL is positively gleaming as it heads north towards Barrowby Road with a train containing Gresley stock in June 1962 – well over a year after its last 'General' at Doncaster Works and a good two months after receiving a Casual Light repair even. The East Coast was fortunate that in the dying years of the steam age, London's fittingly-named 'Top Shed' continued to maintain pride in the job. It is also a tribute to the excellence of the Gresley Pacific design that no fewer than ten of the original twelve built in 1922/23 were still in everyday service when this picture was taken some forty years later! *BLP – E449*.

With touring bicycle lying in the newly-mown hay of the cutting side, an enthusiast (perhaps a friend of the photographer?) relaxes and admires the scene at High Dyke in August 1962 as A3 No.60067 LADAS passes loaded iron ore tipplers in the sidings and nears the end of the climb from Grantham. It will be followed, perhaps, by a freight locomotive sent to High Dyke to collect the valuable orange-coloured payload visible in the wagons and take them north. *BLP – E101.*

On this afternoon in August 1962, visitors to 34F were treated to no fewer than three O2s lined up in a row outside the shed – and all obligingly facing chimney-first. The nearest resident in this 'full house' is O2/2 No.63943, which has not long been out of shops, and behind it are sisters 63941 and 63963, the latter a member of the O2/3 sub-class, which meant that it possessed a more modern side-window cab and reduced boiler mountings. Gresley's 'Consolidations' were generally nicknamed "Tangos" by footplatemen, ostensibly because the dance was popular at about the time they were being introduced . . . but more likely because of their tendency to 'dance' around on the rails and throw their crew about! *BLP – E684.*

The rocky nature of the terrain through which the East Coast Main Line was cut south of Grantham can be appreciated by the foreground in this view of a London-Newcastle express coasting through Saltersford cutting in September 1962. The train is in the charge of A4 No.60028 WALTER K. WHIGHAM and is neatly framed by the now-demolished three-arch bridge. Although it seems at first glance as though the two tracks of the main line are passing through the middle arch, the A4 is actually on the Down main, with the Up slow line on the extreme left. *BLP – E1601.*

With neatly-manicured cutting sides making almost as startling a contrast with the present day as the train itself, V2 2-6-2 No.60862 whistles as it nears the end of its long and arduous climb up Stoke bank with a northbound express in August 1962. In a few moments, the fireman will be able to put his shovel down and relax on the descent into Grantham. Considering there were only eight double-chimneyed V2s altogether, Keith Pirt appears to have been something of a 'magnet' for them. This one, which we also saw on shed on page 70, is one of the scarcest of all, for it is one of only two that had such an exhaust arrangement in combination with outside steam pipes. *BLP – E1222.*

On pages 30/31 can be seen the *ANGLO-SCOTTISH CAR CARRIER* as it appeared in 1960. In this fine study, we see the purpose-built double-decker vehicles that were being deployed in the train by 1962. To the eyes of some enthusiasts, these seemed in a way to almost foretell the Mk3 design of coaches that were to come later in the century (apart from the lack of windows, of course!). This camera angle also shows well the raised silver motif on the side of A4 No.60017 SILVER FOX as it powers through the station with the Up train in August 1962. Although British Rail operated Motorail trains to various national locations in the modern traction era, the concept never really caught on in a major way despite several attempts to resurrect such services over the years. *BLP – E319.*

The presence of major locomotive depots just 28 miles apart at Grantham and Peterborough and the impossibility of rostering balancing turns for every train in the working timetable sometimes required engines to be sent light between the two. In this July 1962 photograph, A3 No.60048 DONCASTER is approaching the Great North Road bridge on the outskirts of Grantham and its crew appear to be taking a great interest in the photographer, the driver having called his mate over to take a look. DONCASTER (which was not, as many have presumed, named after the town or even the railway works but after the winner of the 1873 Derby) was a Grantham engine at the time but would be transferred to Peterborough's New England shed two months afterwards, before returning to the Lincolnshire town the following year to end its career. *BLP – E981.*

To enable readers to make a direct comparison between the A2 and A1 designs, the opportunity has been taken to place two very similar studies alongside each other. On this page is A2/3 No.60500 EDWARD THOMPSON awaiting departure from Grantham's western platform with a northbound train in July 1962. As its name suggests, this was one of the Thompson-designed varieties of Pacific and this particular one was something of a numerical anomaly, for although it was the first of the A2 class, the other batch of A2/3s commenced at 60511, meaning that there were half a dozen A2/2s and four A2/1s in between. Thought of by many LNER aficionados as a rather ungainly-looking machine, EDWARD THOMPSON was not considered a major success by professional railwaymen either and spent the great majority of its life allocated to New England, from where it was often deployed on local semi-fasts and fill-in turns. This meant that it was often seen in Grantham without ever being allocated there. *BLP – E395.*

This fine study of Peppercorn A1 No. 60115 MEG MERRILIES waiting to leave the same platform as the loco on the facing page shows the differences between the design of Arthur Peppercorn and that of his predecessor, Thompson. Immediately obvious is the position of the cylinders, Peppercorn having reverted to Gresley principles on that score . . . and smaller smoke deflectors too. The other big difference, of course, was the fact that A2s had 6ft 2in driving wheels, whereas A1s shared the 6ft 8in size of the A3s and A4s. This photo was taken two months later than the one on the facing page and shows the loco at what was colloquially referred to as 'the Nottingham platform'. In practice, however, the train was far more likely to be headed north towards Newark. *BLP - E359.*

Of the three A2/3 Pacifics that were officially able to call Grantham their 'home', one – No. 60523 SUN CASTLE – has been illustrated on pages 37 and 74. This sister engine, No. 60513 DANTE, was curiously followed around by its younger sibling during its life, for both went new to King's Cross, moved to New England in 1948, moved to Grantham in 1958 and moved back to New England in 1959. Both were condemned there in 1963 and were broken up at Doncaster Works later that year. Here, DANTE is seen running out of Peascliffe tunnel with an up express. The mowing of grass on the cutting sides was necessary in the steam age to prevent lineside fires in bone-dry conditions such as this. *BLP - E587.*

Grantham is one of England's famous 'market towns' and until the end of the 20th century could claim to be so on two fronts – a street market and a cattle market. Unfortunately, the latter has now gone the way of many such establishments and disappeared under a shopping complex. Some of its many pens can be seen in this photograph of A4 No. 60008 DWIGHT D. EISENHOWER leaning to the camber beyond the north end of the station with a down express in August 1962. This Pacific, which until 1945 revelled in the glorious name GOLDEN SHUTTLE, effectively survived – like No. 60010 on page 36 – purely because of its re-naming, being sent by the Government to the United States for preservation at the National Railroad Museum in Green Bay, Wisconsin. As with its North American-based classmate, there have been numerous attempts to repatriate it, but so far without success. *BLP - E774.*

Every book can afford the luxury of one little oddity on its pages and so we thought we'd show you a non-locomotive picture for a change, especially as it provides reference to two of Grantham's greatest industries. The brand new vehicle on 'lowmac' wagon No.E276186 in the Up goods yard in September 1962 is a road-roller built by Aveling-Barford Ltd at its sprawling factory just to the south of there, in the district of Spitalgate. Barfords had a worldwide reputation for steam rollers and other such plant, but, by the time of this photograph, were producing diesel rollers. The factory buildings behind the wagon were part of another huge engineering complex belonging to Ruston & Hornsby, a long-established agricultural machinery and locomotive-building company. *BLP – E1665.*

One of the most commonly-seen A4s at Grantham before it transferred to Scotland was King's Cross favourite No.60034 LORD FARINGDON, which was one of those displaced to New England when 'Top Shed' closed in June 1963, before being sent in October that year to enjoy a famous second career on the Glasgow-Aberdeen route until as late as August 1966. Exactly four years before that, it is pictured climbing through Saltersford cutting on an uncharacteristically-short southbound express. *BLP – E100*.

Once past Stoke signal box, southbound trains were on the four-track 'racing stretch' of the famous Stoke bank and drivers were able to give their steed its head in the hope of an ultra-fast gallop. The aptly-named A4 No.60015 QUICKSILVER has just come over the summit in this pleasing August 1962 scene and is beginning to gain speed, its light grey exhaust trail showing that its fireman is master of his job. QUICKSILVER, introduced in September 1935, was the second-oldest A4. *BLP – E1261*.

As we're almost at the end of the book now, it seems fitting to round off with a portrait of an engine that is now the most famous locomotive in the world, but when Granthamians used to see it on trains like this, it was "just another A3" despite its prior claim to fame as the first steam locomotive in the world to officially achieve a speed of 100 m.p.h. As a member of the King's Cross stud, No.60103 FLYING SCOTSMAN is in immaculate 'just out of the box' condition and makes a superb spectacle as it runs through Spitalgate cutting on the approach to Grantham station in June 1962 – just seven months before its withdrawal and sale to Retford businessman Alan Pegler. But that's another story! *BLP – E530.*

Tailpiece: No, the lad is not hitching a ride on the cab roof of A1 No.60141 ABBOTSFORD as it bursts out of Peascliffe tunnel with a Leeds-King's Cross train in June 1962! Although only a couple of miles outside the town, this was a perfectly peaceful and rural area when Keith Pirt took this picture; today there is an ugly electricity sub-station on the left to supply power to the overhead catenary, the field behind the boy has become a golf course, the wooded ridge in the background has been taken over by large Scandinavian-style holiday lodges and the bridge carrying the once quiet country lane that crossed the line behind the photographer has become a noisy and rather perilous 'rat run' for cars between two busy trunk roads. ABBOTSFORD and her forty-eight sisters never lived to see the changes, all being scrapped in the 1960s, and although a brand new A1 in the form of No.60163 TORNADO has been built and has now passed along this stretch of line several times, there are few people who would disagree with the sentiment that the original locomotives saw the best of it where the railways of Grantham are concerned. The trains may be faster today and much of the original station may still stand, but the vast majority of the infrastructure and the 'ambience of the railway age' has been swept away. Thank heavens for people like Keith Pirt for preserving it all on film for older people to reminisce over and younger people to marvel at. Thanks a million Keith! *BLP – E97.*